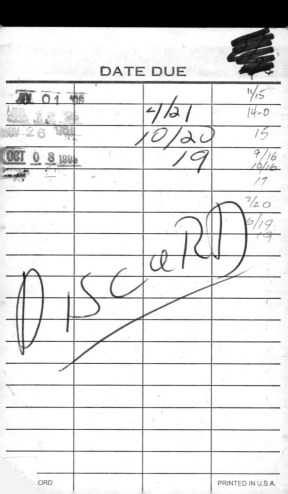

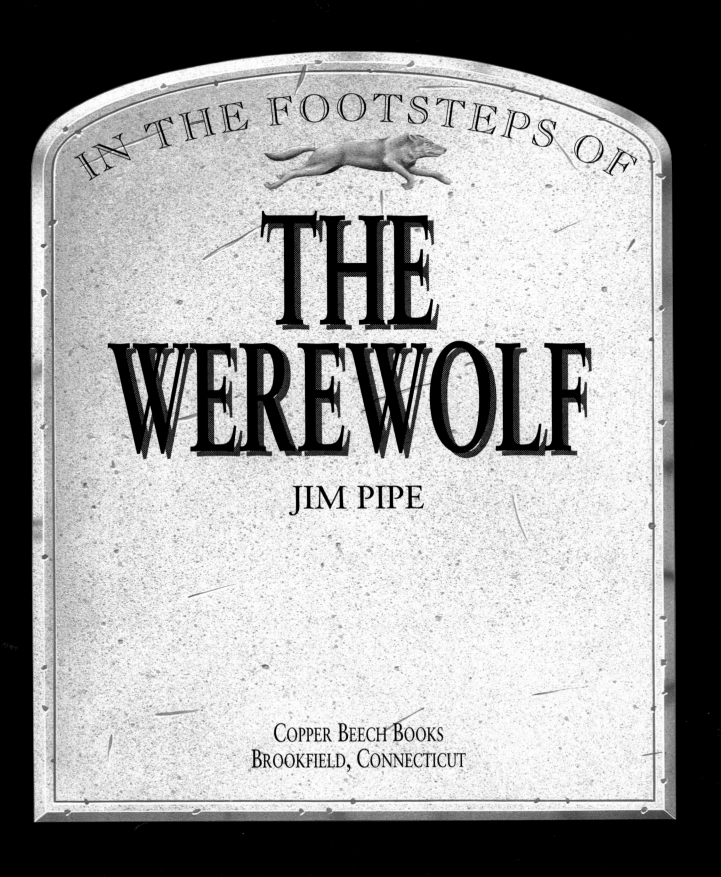

IN THE FOOTSTEPS OF

THE WEREWOLF

JIM PIPE

COPPER BEECH BOOKS
BROOKFIELD, CONNECTICUT

© Aladdin Books Ltd 1996

Designed and produced by
Aladdin Books Ltd
28 Percy Street, London W1P OLD

First published in the United States in 1996 by
Copper Beech Books,
an imprint of The Millbrook Press
2 Old New Milford Road
Brookfield, Connecticut 06804

Editor
Katie Roden
Design
David West Children's Book Design
Designer
Flick Killerby
Picture Research
Brooks Krikler Picture Research
Illustrators
Susanna Addario, Francesca D'Ottavi, Donati Spedaliero – McRae Books, Florence, Italy
Nick Beall – Simon Girling & Associates

Printed in Belgium

Library of Congress Cataloging-in-Publication Data

Pipe, Jim. 1966-
The Werewolf / by Jim Pipe: illustrated by McRae Books Agency.
p. cm.
Includes index.
Summary: The story of the werewolf with tales from ancient times to the Middle Ages.
ISBN 0-7613-0450-9 (lib. bdg.). -- ISBN 0-7613-0465-7 (pbk.)
1. Werewolves--Juvenile literature. [1. Werewolves.] I. Title.
GR830.W4P56 1996   95-39830
398.24'54--dc20
                                          CIP
                                          AC

CONTENTS

The WEREWOLF

That winter, the winds blew stronger than ever, hurling snowflakes against the windows of the small cottage. Inside, an old man sat gently rocking in his chair. He looked sternly at the young faces gathered around him, then spoke these words: "Remember to respect the woods always, children, for who knows what terrible forces are hidden there." The fire crackled behind him, and though the bright orange flames gave off a fierce heat, the old man remained tightly wrapped up in his dog-eared blanket. In fact, none of the children had ever seen their grandfather without that blanket over him. It was as if he never wished his hands to see the light of day.

"So that you never forget the power of the forest," he continued, "I have a story to tell. It is about a young man named Bernard, a bright young fellow, with everything to live for. He was the youngest of three sons, and his mother's favorite. When he reached the age of 17, it was decided that Bernard should go to live with his mother's cousin Otto, to learn his trade as a silversmith. But on the day he left, his mother had a terrible sense of doom. In fact, this was the last time she would ever see him…"

THE WEREWOLF'S CURSE

My chilling tale was born in the dark forests of Germany, home to ancient spirits and forces beyond your human understanding. Read it and shudder at my blood-curdling deeds, wonder at the mysteries of the moon (*below right*), and marvel at the truth about my real-life cousin, the wolf. Meet also the incredible dog-headed tribes of the past (*left*), and the amazing wild children of the forest.

What is a Werewolf?

A werewolf is a man or a woman who can turn into a wolf. The word "werewolf" comes from Anglo-Saxon: *wer* means man, *wulf* is wolf. We are also called *lycanthropes*, and are either true werewolves, as I am, or a weird and horrible version – a human whose wolf skin is furry on the inside!

Tales of the Wolf

When G.W.M. Reynolds wrote *Wagner the Wehr-Wolf* in 1846, it became an instant hit (*below*). Eighty-seven years later, Guy Endore wrote the classic tale *The Werewolf of Paris* (1933), and the werewolf has lived on in many movies.

The legend is actually one of the oldest human superstitions. Reports of werewolves came mainly from the countryside. As towns spread, werewolf stories started to disappear. Perhaps werewolves just became more cunning. Who can tell...

The Werewolf

Bernard had heard the stories about the forest and the terrifying beasts said to lurk there. But as he strolled along the path, nothing could have been further from his mind. He whistled happily, thinking of what life would be like in the bustling market town on the other side of the forest.

As he walked into the forest, however, fear took a grip on his mind. The trees seemed to huddle together as if in ambush, and the sunlight struggled to find a way through the thick branches. The wind played tricks on his eyes as it stirred the dead leaves on the ground.

Suddenly, there was a rustling in the bushes. Bernard stopped, his heart pounding. The faint noise became the snarling sound of a savage beast, and a brown streak carved a path through the undergrowth. In a flash, Bernard was knocked off his feet...

AN ANCIENT MYTH

Stories of werewolves have terrified humans since history began. They have appeared among the ancient Sumerians and Romans (*right*), the Navajo Indians, and the Vikings of Europe.

The Cult of Lycaon

According to the Greek writer Pausanias (c. A.D. 400), the wooded slopes of Mount Lycaeus were home to a strange cult who sacrificed humans to the sky god, Zeus. One of the people watching the

bloody spectacle would be turned into a wolf and forced to wander the earth for nine years. If he avoided eating human flesh during that time, he could regain his human shape.

This ritual originated from the myth of King Lycaon of Arcadia, who had sacrificed a baby to Zeus and was instantly changed into a wolf for his crime. Pausanias also tells of a Greek boxer (*above*) named Damarchus, who won an Olympic victory in about 400 B.C. after changing into a wolf and back again!

A Norse Werewolf

The Viking saga *Volsungasaga* tells of a father and son, Sigmund and Sinfjotli, who one day came across a hut in the forest. Inside were two men with strange looking gold rings on their fingers.

Above the men hung two wolf skins. Sigmund and Sinfjotli put them on and instantly became wolves who only returned to human form every tenth half-day. After many exploits, the pair finally burned the skins so that the curse would be broken.

The monster knocked the young man to the ground. Bernard closed his eyes and waited for the pain of a gruesome death. He smelled the foul breath of the creature on his face and then – the warm, sticky sensation of a huge tongue licking his forehead! Opening his eyes, he saw that the beast was just a big, friendly dog.

A hand stretched out to help and, as Bernard looked up, his eyes met those of a hunter. Her grip was strong and, as she helped Bernard to his feet, she smiled warmly.

"I'm sorry," she said, "we don't meet many people out here, so Molly here can get a bit excited. Where are you going?"

"Olburg," replied Bernard, "I'm going to work with my Uncle Otto."

"Olburg? Then make sure you reach town by nightfall. Evil dwells in this forest and, when the moon is full, danger is everywhere."

Without another word, she whistled to the dog and the pair vanished into the trees, as suddenly as they had appeared.

MEDIEVAL WEREWOLVES

After the Black Death, when a third of its population died of a mystery disease, medieval Europe was a place of fear and superstition. With fewer people around, wolves again ruled the forests of Europe.

These terrifying creatures became a symbol of all that was unknown and feared. As well as believing in werewolf myths, people thought that foreign tribes, known as *cynocephali*, had wolf heads (*right*)! But, as the following two stories show, not all werewolves were evil.

The Magic Plant of Gorgalon

A magic plant growing in the garden of King Gorgalon turned any person who cut it into a wolf. Gorgalon's treacherous queen tricked him into cutting the stem, and he was forced to flee to a distant forest. Here he met a local king who, amazed by the speaking wolf, spared his life. Soon they became friends (*left*), and the king later forced the queen to restore Gorgalon to his human form.

Alphonse the Werewolf

In a French story written around 1194–1197, Prince Alphonse of Spain was turned into a werewolf by his wicked stepmother, using a magic ointment. As a wolf, Alphonse saved the young Prince of Sicily, Guillaume, from a plot to kill him. The pair were chased across Sicily, but the wolf ferried the boy across the Straits of Messina to Italy (*right*).

Many years later, Guillaume returned to Sicily to defeat his enemies. Alphonse was restored to human form when a red cord with a magic ring was tied around his neck.

Bernard was puzzled by the mysterious woman with the deep brown eyes and chestnut-colored hair. What had she meant by "danger?" Surely someone who knew the forest as she did would have no time for foolish tales of magic and monsters. Turning these thoughts over in his mind, Bernard stepped off the path without noticing. He was soon hopelessly lost in the labyrinth of trees.

Bernard vainly sought the path, at first impatiently, then frantically. The light dimmed, and a thick mist settled over the forest. All was dark, except for the glint of a full moon through the trees.

The silence of the forest was shattered by the blood-curdling howl of a wolf. Bernard froze. He had to escape – but where to? In the distance he heard the voices of a hunting party, and he started to run toward their flickering torches. And then – Wham!

Great jaws snapped at Bernard's throat and razor-sharp claws ripped at his chest. Then everything went black...

THE BIG HUNT

The 16th century was the golden age of the werewolf. In lonely villages nestled in the mountains of France and Germany, thousands were accused of attacking people while in werewolf form. Today, it seems incredible that no one ever suspected a real wolf of the attacks!

The Beast of Cologne

All of Europe knew the story of Peter Stubb (*left and below*), who was tried in 1589. Stubb was said to own a magic belt, which changed him into "a greedy devouring wolf, strong and mighty, with eyes great and large, which in the night sparkled like brands of fire."

Stubb was accused of attacking travelers on lonely country roads. His captors said that their pack of dogs had been attacking a large wolf, which changed into a man and escaped from the pack. Stubb was brought before the local magistrate, then tortured horribly. He confessed to being a werewolf and, although his magic belt was never found, he was beheaded and his body was burned at the stake.

Bernard woke to the sounds of the forest. What *had* happened the night before? His clothes were soaked in blood, but he had no wounds or scars. And what was the beast that had attacked him?

Bernard washed his torn, bloody shirt in a nearby stream, then followed the running water in the hopes that it might lead him back to the path. Sure enough it did, and in two hours he had reached Olburg. Entering the town square, he heard shouting and commotion and saw a large crowd gathered around the body of a naked man strung between two poles. More people were lighting a bonfire.

Then a voice cried, "Why, if it isn't young Bernard!" It was Uncle Otto. He clapped Bernard on the back, then whispered: "Try to forget what you have seen. It is the Devil's work. Last night a werewolf was shot, and we must burn its human form to rid ourselves of its curse." As he spoke, the great bonfire ignited with a mighty roar.

FROM HUMAN TO WOLF

So how do you know if someone is a werewolf? Useful clues to look for are anyone with pointed ears, hair on the palms of their hands, curved fingernails, and eyebrows that meet in the middle! But the eyes of the werewolf stay the same, whether it is in human or wolf form.

Beware of the Full Moon!

In films (but not legend), werewolves are created by a spoken curse. In the 1913 movie *The Werewolf*, the curse went:

Even a man who is pure in heart
And says his prayers by night
Can become the wolf when the wolfbane blooms
And the autumn moon is bright.

Five Ways To Become A Werewolf

All werewolf legends have one thing in common – the best time for a transformation is in the light of the full moon. Exactly how this happens depends on where the legend comes from. Here are five common ways to transform yourself:

🐺 Smearing yourself with the fat of a newly killed cat mixed with aniseed, wearing a belt made from wolf's skin (*above*), then chanting a tribute to the wolf spirit!

🐺 Eating part of a sheep killed by a wolf.

🐺 Drinking water from a wolf's footprints.

🐺 Getting thrown out of church in medieval Normandy, France.

🐺 Being a witch – some Europeans thought witches could become werewolves.

Despite his uncle's words, Bernard could not forget what he had seen. Although its body had turned to ashes in the heat of the fire, the beast lived on in his nightmares.

During the day Bernard was kept busy learning Uncle Otto's trade. But each night, as he lay alone in his bed, he imagined a silver-haired monster waiting in the dark corners of his room, ready to leap out from the shadows and rip out his heart.

Otto's fair-haired daughter, Rebecca, sensed that something was troubling Bernard but was afraid to ask. So when the traveling circus came to Olburg two weeks later, she led him to a brightly colored tent on the edge of the camp. Peering into the darkness within, Bernard saw a shadowy, mysterious woman.

"Do not be afraid, young man," she said, "for I can answer the questions you long to ask." But as she gazed into the swirling mists of the crystal ball, the woman's face turned white with terror.

With a ghastly screech, she fled from the tent, and Bernard was left alone with the crystal ball – and the image of the wolf...

CRYING WOLF!

Much of the terror of the werewolf comes from a human fear of the wolf itself. A few stories tell us about the gentle side of the wolf, as in the Roman myth of Romulus and Remus being brought up by a she-wolf (*left*). But in most tales, such as the story of the *Three Little Pigs*, the wolf is a bloodthirsty killer.

Destruction of the Wolf

There have been few genuine reports of wolf attacks on humans. But the wolf has always been a threat to domestic animals like sheep, so it soon became a symbol of evil. Special hunters, like King Charlemagne of France's *luporii*, were paid to kill only wolves (*right*).

   In the laws of some countries, knights had to spend every Saturday hunting wolves. By the end of the 15th century, the wolf had been almost wiped out in Europe.

The Beast of Gevaudan

In 1765, a great wolf burst into a group of children playing near the village of Villaret, France. The wolf seized one child, but the others beat it off with sticks and stones (*left*). The wolf returned, however, and in two years killed over 60 people without being caught! It is easy to see why local people thought such a ferocious beast could have supernatural powers.

Although he was deeply shocked by what he had seen in the crystal ball, Bernard did not mention it to Rebecca. And as the days passed, the world around him gradually changed.

Bernard's senses tingled as Olburg seemed to explode into strong colors, sounds, and smells. A quiet heartbeat became a beating drum, the delicate scent of his uncle's roses turned into a powerful odor, and a distant bird looked like a blaze of bright color. His body had never felt so alive, yet it also felt so strange.

Bernard's dreams changed, too. The gruesome wolf was gone, replaced by the sights and sounds of the forest. When he awoke each morning, Bernard could smell cool forest air in his nostrils and feel damp grass beneath his feet – and hands.

At the same time, Otto noticed how clumsy his nephew had become. It seemed as if the silver was burning his hands. But had he looked closer, his concern would have turned to fear: Thick black hair had begun to sprout from Bernard's palms!

THE BIG BAD WOLF

If the werewolves of legend are supposedly humans in wolf form, then just how like real wolves are they?

Just a Big Dog?

The wolf is one of the largest members of the dog family, though they have longer legs, a wider head, and a long, bushy tail. Adult wolves weigh about 100 pounds and are between 5 to 6 feet long. There are many types of wolf, such as the timber wolf, the Arctic wolf, and the desert wolf, but the gray wolf is the most common. Wolves can live in almost any climate, from harsh Arctic conditions to the blazing heat of the desert.

One Happy Family

Unlike werewolves, who are usually said to hunt alone, wolves like to live in groups called *packs*. The wolf pack is led by a strong male and female. A pack can live in an area of 400 sq miles, because wolves can travel 30 miles in a day. This area is fiercely defended and any lone wolves caught trespassing are killed. Cubs *(top)* are looked after by both parents and helper wolves, who teach them how to hunt.

Arctic wolf

Timber wolf

Walking through the square, Bernard spotted Maria, the hunter he had met in the forest. Last time, Maria's dog had been happy to see him; now, she growled. "What's up Molly?" joked Maria, "Have you seen a werewolf?" But looking again at Bernard, she sensed that something was wrong.

That night, the full moon shone brightly as Bernard went for a stroll outside the town walls. Suddenly, his whole body shook and his stomach felt as if it was about to explode. Gasping in agony, he fell to the ground. His body jerked from side to side, helpless against the forces that gripped him.

Bernard tried to scream, but no sound came from his lips. His face had split in two to reveal huge, gaping jaws. The sound of cracking bones filled the air as his arms and legs stretched to form mighty limbs. His back bulged horribly, and thick hairs spread like worms across his entire body. The wolf in Bernard had come alive! It threw back its great head, and let out a dreadful howl...

THE CALL OF THE WILD

The howl of the werewolf Bernard would be enough to send shivers down most people's spines. But for real wolves, it is an important means of getting in touch with their friends.

Wolf Communication

Unlike werewolves, who don't usually stay for a chat, wolves communicate with each other in lots of different ways – howling, sniffing, and licking each other's coats. If you ever bump into a wolf, you can tell if it's angry by looking at its face (*below*)!

furious!   *angry*   *afraid*   *terrified*

Tail positions can also show how a wolf is feeling. For example, if a wolf's tail is between its legs (*top*), it is afraid. And while werewolves only enjoy killing, wolves also like to play. Their teeth are razor sharp, but wolves rarely hurt each other while playing.

A wolf's howl can last for up to 20 seconds.

Howl Do They Do That?

When howling, a wolf holds up its head and lays back its ears. Wolves can howl for hours, and every wolf has a characteristic "voice." Wolves howl for many different reasons:

- To make contact with others in their pack;
- To call a pack meeting;
- Because they are lonely!

A brisk wind whistled through the trees as the wolf forced its way through the thick undergrowth, its yellow eyes glowing like hot coals in the forest gloom. Every now and then it snarled savagely, and startled birds cried in alarm as they flew off into the night.

Half a mile away, the white coats of a herd of sheep shone in the silvery moonlight, a beacon to the monster in the valley below. They munched happily, unaware of the ferocious beast that stalked them.

For a brief moment, all was quiet as the werewolf neared its prey. Then, with a tremendous burst of speed, the huge creature fell upon an unlucky sheep that had strayed from the flock. In one quick movement, the werewolf grasped the sheep's neck in its vicelike jaws, lifted it off the ground and tossed it to one side, ripping its throat.

The werewolf stood over its dying victim and watched as the rest of the herd scattered in panic. Then, throwing back its head, it howled in savage triumph.

THE HUNTER

Werewolves have a simple diet of sheep and humans. Wolves, however, will eat anything to stay alive, from deer (*below*), rabbits, and rats, to large insects and worms! When meat is scarce, they will even eat fruit and buds.

Hunting Techniques

Despite all the tales of savage attacks on humans (*left*), few unprovoked wolf attacks have ever been proved.

Wolves actually choose to avoid humans, though they watch our movements closely. Scientists have noticed that in winter they even make use of roads cleared by snowplows! Near towns they wait until night falls, then come into town to rummage through the garbage for food.

Grandma, What Big Teeth You Have!

The size of a wolf pack often depends on prey in the region. It takes 20 Arctic wolves to kill a musk ox, while a white-tailed deer takes 10. Wolves kill with a series of bites, though bigger animals are usually bitten just on the throat. To save energy, wolves prey on the young and the old. So the story of *Little Red Riding Hood (left)* does have some truth in it.

The following morning, a horrified shepherd discovered the bloody remains of one of his sheep. On the other side of the valley, Bernard awoke shivering in the cold air. Someone had stolen his clothes! What was he doing in the forest...and why was he wet? Looking down, he gasped in horror – he was soaked with blood from head to toe. What had happened last night? The last thing he could remember was a terrible pain.

Bernard scrubbed himself with leaves to remove as much of the blood as possible, then crept toward the town walls. It was still early, but a woman and her son were washing sheets in a nearby stream. Bernard waited until their backs were turned, then snatched a sheet from their clothesline as it blew toward him.

Wrapping his cold, naked body in the damp linen, Bernard ran quickly to the town gate. A sleeping sentry lay slumped against the gate. Had he been awake, he would have been terrified by the bloody, ghostlike figure that slipped quietly past.

THE WOLF TODAY

Today, wolves are beginning to return to their original haunts in the mountains and forests of Europe. After humans, the gray wolf is now the most widespread of all large land mammals. It can be found in Europe, the Middle East, India, Asia, and North America. You never know, there might soon be one living near you!

The End of the Wolf – But Not Quite!

At one point, it looked as if the wolf would never live in Europe or the United States again. The last surviving wolf in the United Kingdom was shot in 1726, and in France in 1927. But their legendary cunning and natural shyness helped a few wolves to survive. Many migrated to the harsh, lonely climates of Siberia and Canada, and are now slowly returning to their old hunting grounds.

Who's Afraid of the Big Bad Wolf?

Many people, especially farmers, are shocked that the wolf is being encouraged to return to places like Montana, the Abruzzi hills in Italy, and the Highlands of Scotland. In Spain, some motorists deliberately run wolves down because they are protected by law and cannot be shot.

In an age when humans have little to fear from the wolf, its reputation still causes terror and anger. In many people's minds, it is still the "big bad wolf," the night prowler on the lookout for small children to gobble up!

When he reached home, Bernard climbed the wall of the house next door. With a wolf's strength and agility, he leaped from the rooftop, grasped the ledge, and swung into his bedroom. He bundled the bloody sheet under his bed, then quickly washed himself.

At breakfast, Otto mentioned that another sheep had been slaughtered. Bernard knew then that his dreams were a terrifying reality. He was a werewolf!

A month passed, and each night Bernard waited in terror for the agony of transformation. Nothing happened, but he felt the wolf inside him growing stronger. When the next full moon arrived, he went to an inn, hoping that a drunken werewolf could harm no one.

As the clock struck midnight, a searing pain ripped through his body. Knocking into tables, he staggered out into the night.

THE MOON

The strange nature of the moon has always linked it to supernatural forces. Mysteriously, ocean tides rise and fall in rhythm with the moon. Unlike the sun, it constantly grows (*waxes*) or shrinks (*wanes*).

The moon goes around the earth at the same speed as the earth's rotation, so no human saw the dark side of the moon until a Soviet space mission in 1959.

Full Moon

Waxing/waning Moon

New Moon

Early Observers

Early astronomers thought the moon was flat because there were no shadows around the edges. They did not realize that the surface is uniformly lit because of its texture. The first moon map

was drawn by William Gilbert, a doctor to Elizabeth I of England, in 1600. After the invention of the telescope by Galileo (1564–1642), accurate maps were drawn by Giambattista Riccioli (1598–1671), who thought that the dark areas were dried seabeds! They are still known as seas today.

The Men in the Moon

Until the mid-18th century, even scientists believed that the moon was inhabited by strange creatures called *lunarians* (*right*). As late as 1822, F.P. Gruithuisen, a German astronomer, claimed to have discovered a "lunar city!"

ernard dragged his body into the forest, trying to get as far from the inn as possible before he changed. But his drunkenness sent the wolf within him into a foaming rage. With saliva dribbling from his massive jaws, the wolf went in search of blood – human blood.

Bernard had been laughing and joking with two travelers at the inn. Puzzled by his departure, they had finished their drinks and set off for Olburg. Little did they expect to meet him again so soon – and in such a guise.

The two men walked lazily through the forest, guided by the lights of the town. They heard nothing as a huge shape moved swiftly through the shadows behind them.

In an instant, the wolf had pounced on them, stunning one with a single blow before hurling himself at the other. The traveler fought bravely, but he stood no chance against the whirling blur of bloody fangs and claws.

MOON MYTHOLOGY

To early civilizations, the moon was the land of the gods and a resting place for the souls of the dead. In many cultures it was represented by a goddess, such as the Native American Athenesic (*right*) and the Chinese Chang-O. The Romans wore moon amulets to improve their fertility and protect themselves when traveling.

The Gory Hand Of Glory

Several centuries ago, the "hand of glory" was said to be a fiendish tool used by robbers. To create it, they cut off the right hand of a murderer during an eclipse of the moon. The hand was wrapped in a shroud, squeezed dry of blood, and pickled in a mixture of saltpeter, salt and pepper. It was then dipped in wax and the fingers lit with candles (*left*). Once lit, it made the occupants of a house fall asleep while the robbers went to work.

Other Moon Magic

The actual extent of the moon's influence on humans is not known for certain, but for thousands of years it has been blamed for people's strange behavior *(left)*. The word lunatic, for example, comes from the Latin word for moon, *luna*.

In a pack of tarot cards, used for fortune telling, the moon card (*right*) represents the forces of nature and the unconscious. However, if you believe in the power of a full moon, and you expect trouble, you'll probably help to make trouble happen!

LA·LUNE

The unfortunate woman who found the two travelers fainted when she saw what remained of their bodies. Within an hour, the whole town was talking about nothing else. From now on, only the foolish and the brave left the safety of the town walls to go into the forest.

Killing a sheep was bad enough, but the deaths of the two men devastated Bernard. He had to find a way to break the curse. So, pretending that he needed to visit his mother, Bernard traveled to Gramfurt, a city famed for its university.

For two weeks he stalked the library, reading ancient books so long untouched that they were almost buried in dust. But not one gave him the clues to breaking the curse of the werewolf.

Bernard returned to Olburg to say farewell to Rebecca and Otto. He knew what the next full moon would bring – and this time, the townspeople would be waiting for him.

TO KILL A WEREWOLF

Bernard didn't have much luck at the library, but if you want to get rid of a werewolf, what can you do? First, track it down to its den, perhaps by following a trail of blood from a kill (*left*). The werewolf favors lonely places, and powerful werewolves hunt by both day and night.

Breaking the Curse

A werewolf's prey remains a werewolf forever. It is doomed to wander the world until it is killed by a silver bullet or, in some legends, pierced between the eyebrows with a pitchfork (*right*).

Once you have killed a werewolf, you should cut off its head, then burn it and the body. Then the ashes must be scattered to make sure that the curse is fully broken.

A Werewolf Hunting Kit

In addition to an incredible amount of bravery, a werewolf hunter will need:

- Holy water, blessed by a priest – some werewolves are afraid of this.
- A pistol – make sure you have a good supply of silver bullets!
- A pitchfork – just in case you run out of bullets.
- An axe – to cut off a werewolf's head after it is dead.
- A knife – to defend yourself by cutting off its paws.

Over the past months, Rebecca had begun to fall in love with Bernard. But in the back of her mind, she felt that he was always hiding something from her. While he was away, she discovered the bloody sheet in his room. Could this explain his strange behavior?

Rebecca had no time to question her cousin, however. It was the day of the full moon, and Bernard had run deep into the forest, praying that nobody would dare to leave the town. But two herdsmen, driving their sheep far from their village in search of fresh pastures, knew nothing of the Beast of Olburg, as the werewolf was now known.

The wolf had butchered half their flock before the shepherds arrived with their knives. The monster leaped up, and soon one shepherd lay dead, his head crushed by a single blow of the beast's paw.

The other was bigger and stronger. Slashing with his knife, he cut off one of the wolf's paws. The beast ran off, howling with pain. When Bernard awoke the next morning, his left hand was nothing but a bloody stump!

A SECOND SKIN

From the earliest times, humans wore wolf skins to give the wearer the savage nature of the beast (*left*). Could these have been the real werewolves – people who became ferocious because they thought they had turned into animals?

A Wolf in Wolf's Clothing

Not only wolf skins were worn for courage and ferocity. Hunters from the Bronze Age (6000 B.C.) village of Catal Huyuk wrapped leopard skins around their waists, and Inuits from the far north of what is now Canada wore polar bear skins. In Africa, followers of the Cult of the Leopard wore the skins, teeth, and "claws" of leopards *(below right)* to strike fear into their victims before murdering them.

Utterly Berserk!

Equally terrifying were the Berserkers (from the Scandinavian word *berr*, meaning naked). These Viking warriors *(below left)* wore bear and wolf skins and took drugs to lose control of themselves. They were also famed for their howling, which could make their enemies' hair stand on end!

Bernard returned to the house.

He crept into his room, to find Rebecca waiting. "My secret is out," he cried. "You must despise the beast that lurks beneath my skin. I should have killed myself long ago, but now the wolf within me is too strong. Kill me, I beg you."

"No," replied Rebecca, "there must be a cure. Hide in the cellar, or your missing hand will give you away. Let me tend to your wound."

The night of the full moon approached and, terrified of the monster that Bernard would become, Rebecca chained him to the cellar walls. Outside, armed gangs roamed the streets, looking for the owner of the bloody hand that the shepherd had brought into town.

Uncle Otto was busy too, crafting silver bullets for Maria to use to kill the werewolf. If he had only known that, at that very moment, the werewolf was hiding in his damp cellar, living off the scraps that Rebecca stole from his table.

A VERY WILD CHILD

One explanation for the legend of the werewolf can be found in the extraordinary cases of abandoned children who have survived in the wild, known as *feral children*.

Victor of Aveyron

In 1797, people from a village in the French region of Aveyron became frightened by a mysterious "wild man" seen running through the nearby forest. Three years later, the villagers finally captured a naked twelve-year-old boy, who was covered with cuts and bruises and terrified of other humans.

No one ever found out how Victor had been abandoned, for despite the efforts of a young doctor, Jean Marc Itard, he never learned to speak. His skin was so tough he could hold burning wood without feeling any pain, and he preferred to eat nuts and berries to any prepared food. His story was made into a film (*top*).

Children of the Wolf

Edgar Rice Burroughs' character Tarzan, raised by apes in the African jungle (*left*), was fictional. Yet many real-life children have been found in the wild.

Sixteen children were found in India alone in 1843–1933. Perhaps they were the inspiration for Mowgli (*above*), the wolf-child in Rudyard Kipling's story *The Jungle Book*. One Dutch boy, found in 1863, lived off birds. He would imitate their call, climb trees, and eat any birds or eggs that he found!

Ever since that first kill, Bernard had felt the power and energy of the wolf pulsing through his veins. At first it had been exciting, but now the vicious nature of the beast was affecting his mind.

Looking at him, Rebecca could barely recognize the happy, hopeful youth who had arrived just a few months earlier. Thick hair sprouted from his pale face, and his body had grown lean and hard.

Bernard again pleaded with Rebecca to kill him. But she refused to give in. Someone must be able to help them. And then it came to her – the fortune-teller who had fled screaming from the tent! Rebecca saddled her father's horse and galloped off in search of the circus. After three desperate days, she finally caught up with it.

She begged the fortune-teller to help her lift the werewolf's curse. "I want nothing to do with that evil beast," the woman said. But when she saw the love in Rebecca's eyes, she gave in. She handed her a small glass bottle containing an inky solution. "Give your friend this herbal cure on the stroke of midnight. Now hurry, for tomorrow brings the full moon."

ALL IN THE MIND?

Some experts believe that lycanthropy can be explained as a disease. There have been some remarkable cases of men and women (*right*) with incredibly thick body hair, but this didn't make them werewolves any more than people with very little hair! A better argument is that some people believe they are wolves and so start to behave like them.

The Animal Spirit

Under the influence of drugs, the Berserkers (page 31) certainly thought they were wolves. Horror stories such as R.L. Stephenson's *Dr. Jekyll and Mr. Hyde* show that everybody has a good and a bad side, and the fact that drugs can bring out extremes in our personality (*left*). Lycanthropy is possible without drugs – victims believe they are wolves to the point where they prowl around at night, their skin becomes pale, and they are constantly thirsty.

A Mystery Disease?

One theory is that an extremely rare form of the disease porphyria may have condemned innocent sufferers to death at the hands of werewolf hunters.

The disease turns the skin yellow and the teeth red, and creates growths that can badly distort the face. But, as the tale of *Beauty and the Beast* points out (*right*), looks tell us nothing about the person inside!

Rebecca rode like the wind, urging her horse onward. But it was too late. As she reached the edge of the forest, the clock struck the first of its twelve chimes. The chains that held Bernard shattered as the werewolf exploded from his body. The monster bounded up the cellar steps and smashed through the heavy oak door at the top.

Terrified people ran here, there, and everywhere as the werewolf pounded toward the town gate. Only Maria stood firm, waiting with a hunter's patience for the right moment to fire. But as the werewolf came into view, there was something so familiar about the look in its eyes that she hesitated for one brief moment. The werewolf howled as the shot hit its hind leg, and headed out toward the forest.

Maria and a few braver members of the crowd chased after the limping monster. Just then, Rebecca rode up. "Don't shoot," she cried, "I've got the cure!" But Maria had already pulled out her pistol. She would not miss a second time. Taking aim, she squeezed the trigger...

AT THE MOVIES

Since 1913, the werewolf has terrified audiences in over 50 films, played by great actors like Henry Hull, Lon Chaney Jr., and Oliver Reed (*bottom*). Many ran around on two feet, and today their makeup sometimes looks anything but scary!

An Oscar for the Wolf

By the 1980s, special robotic devices and the latest cosmetic techniques brought a new realism to the monster in the film *An American Werewolf in London* (1983, *top right*), which won an Oscar for makeup. Similar effects were used in *Wolf*, the 1994 film starring Jack Nicolson.

The New Breed

The story of the werewolf has also inspired films like *Cat People* (1983), in which the heroine turns into a huge panther (*middle right*). In *Spiderman*, Peter Parker is bitten by a radioactive spider and gains the ability to climb walls and spin webs (*bottom right*)!

When the smoke of the gunpowder cleared, Maria saw the beast towering over Rebecca. The sight of the monster had made Rebecca's horse rear, and the bullet destined for the werewolf's heart had hit the horse instead. It had fallen to the ground, trapping Rebecca's leg.

The crowd waited breathlessly for the beast to pounce. But the werewolf gave Rebecca one last look then leaped into the forest, snarling. It was never seen again.

"So, children," said the grandfather, "next time you are out in the forest, remember never to stray from the path. Now, I think it's time you all went to bed, so leave this old man to put out the fire and lock the doors." The children kissed their grandfather, then howled at each other playfully as they scampered up the stairs.

The old man smiled and walked across to the fireplace, letting his blanket drop to the floor. He strained to push the heavy iron grate into place. "This would be so much easier," he thought to himself, "if only I had my left hand instead of this stump."

THE WORLD OF THE WOLF

Cynocephali – Despite the journeys of explorers like Marco Polo, medieval people still believed that the edge of the world was populated by strange peoples. Among these were the *cynocephali*, meaning "dog-headed people" in Greek.

Feral Children – This term describes children who are born or who live in the wild without human contact.

Full moon – A full moon happens once a month, when the entire face of the moon is lit up by the sun.

Lunar eclipse – In a lunar eclipse, the moon passes through the shadow of the earth. The moon changes color and can seem to disappear (some cultures thought the world was going to end!)

Lunarians – Up until the last century, many scientists believed that creatures called *lunarians* lived on the moon. Since the moon landings we have known that life cannot exist on the moon's surface.

Luporii – This is the name given to King Charlemagne's specialized huntsmen who were trained to track and kill wolves.

Lycanthropy – From the Greek words meaning "wolf man," this term is now used by doctors to describe people who genuinely believe that they are werewolves. However, the word "lycanthrope" is also used to mean werewolves in myth and legend.

Saltpeter – The traditional name for potassium nitrate.

Shape-shifting – This is a term for the transformation of humans into animals, such as leopards (Africa), foxes (Japan), and wolves (Europe and America).

Wolfsbane – A plant containing drugs that may have made people think they had turned into animals. However, it probably got its name because the deadly poison extracted was used to tip the arrows of ancient wolf-hunters.

INDEX

Photocredits (*Abbreviations: t–top, m–middle, b–bottom, r–right, l–left*)
4, 5b, 15t, 21t & b, 25 both, 26, 27br, 31 – Mary Evans Picture Library; 5t, 7 both, 9, 13, 15m – Ancient Art & Architecture Collection; 6, 17 both, 19, 21m, 23m, 24, 39 – Bruce Coleman Collection; 11tr – engraving by Jacques Callot; 11b, 27ml, 29, 35t – Fortean Picture Library; 23t & b – NHPA; 30 – Hulton Deutsch; 33t – The Ronald Grant Archive; 33b – Frank Spooner Pictures; 35m & b – Kobal Collection; 37t – Polygram/Universal Pictures (courtesy Kobal); 37m – Universal Pictures (courtesy Kobal); 37br – Columbia Pictures (courtesy Kobal); 37bl – Hammer Films (courtesy Kobal); 38 – Roger Vlitos.